READY - TO - PLAY

17 CONTEMPORARY CHRISTIAN HITS
VOLUME FOUR

EASY PIANO ARRANGEMENTS
BY DAVID THIBODEAUX

www.brentwoodbenson.com

BRENTWOOD-BENSON
music publishing

CONTENTS

Adonai

Words and Music by
STEPHANIE LEWIS, LORRAINE FERRO
and DON KOCH
Arranged by David Thibodeaux

4

Back in His Arms Again

Words and Music by
MARK SCHULTZ
Arranged by David Thibodeaux

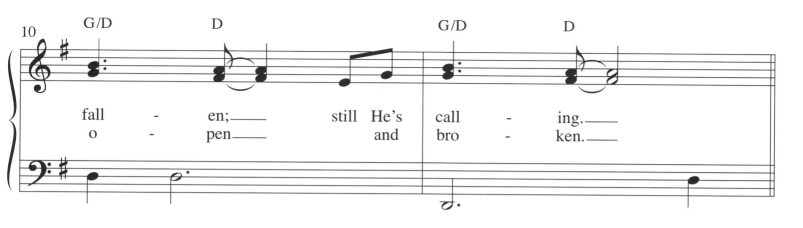

10

G/D   D   G/D   D

fall - en;_____ still He's   call - ing._____
o - pen_____ and   bro - ken._____

12

G

'Cause I be - lieve that He loves you where_____ you

13

D/F♯

are. I be - lieve that you've seen the hands_____ of

14

Em

God. I be - lieve that you'll know it when you're

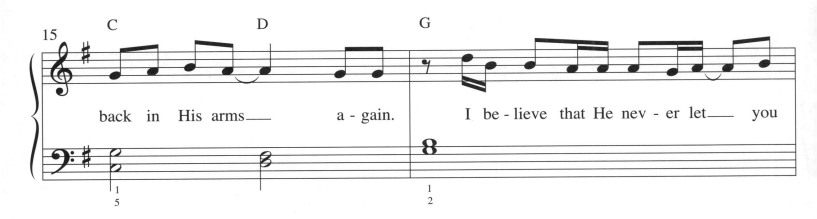

back in His arms—— a - gain. I be - lieve that He nev - er let—— you

go. I be - lieve that He's want - ing you—— to

3rd time to Coda ⊕

know. I be - lieve that He'll lead you 'til you're

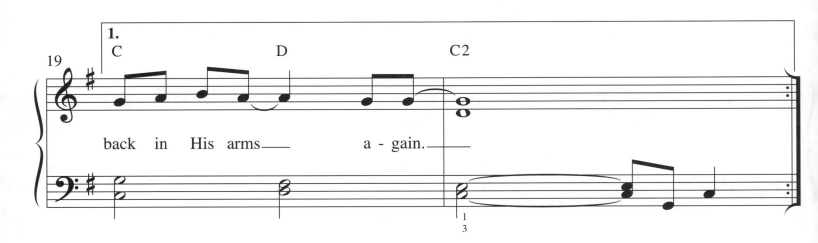

back in His arms—— a - gain.——

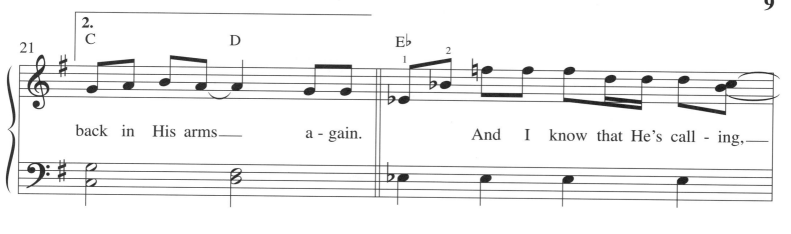

back in His arms___ a - gain. And I know that He's call - ing,___

___ He's call-ing you home.

D.S. al Coda

CODA

back in His arms,___ you're back in His arms,___

back in His arms___ a - gain.

Alive

Words and Music by
MATT BRONLEEWE and REBECCA ST. JAMES
Arranged by David Thibodeaux

Lyrics:

1. I al-ways want-ed to be free 'til I was bound. And then I al-ways want-ed my own way
2. I used to think that me, my-self, and I were all that mat-tered. But You've shown me all this world can give

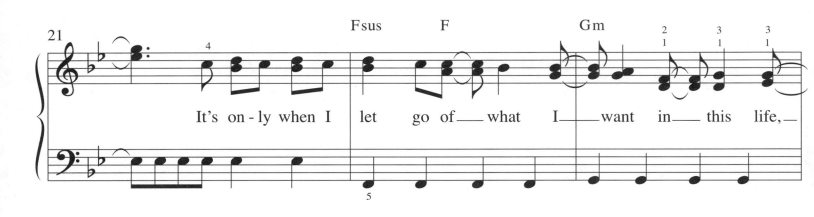

It's on-ly when I let go of what I want in this life,

You make me come a-

3rd time to Coda

live.

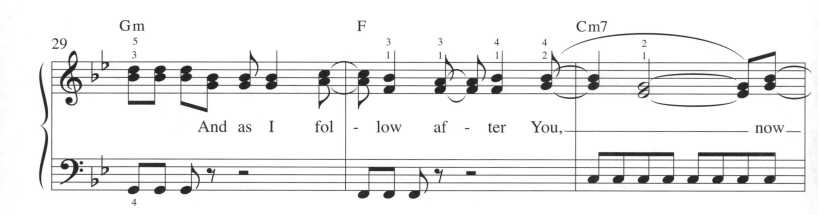

And as I fol-low af-ter You, now

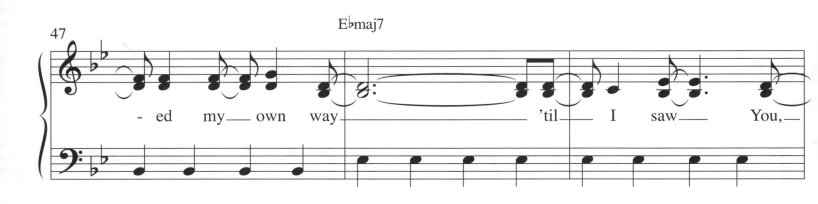

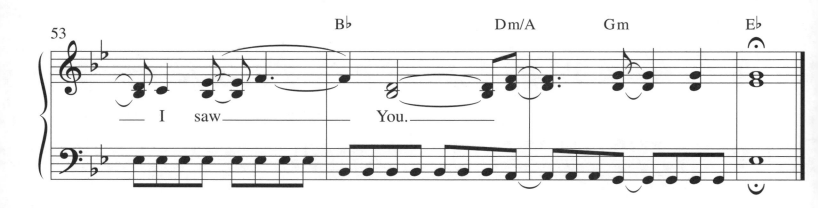

Cry Out to Jesus

Words and Music by
MAC POWELL, DAVID CARR,
TAI ANDERSON and BRAD AVERY / MARK LEE
Arranged by David Thibodeaux

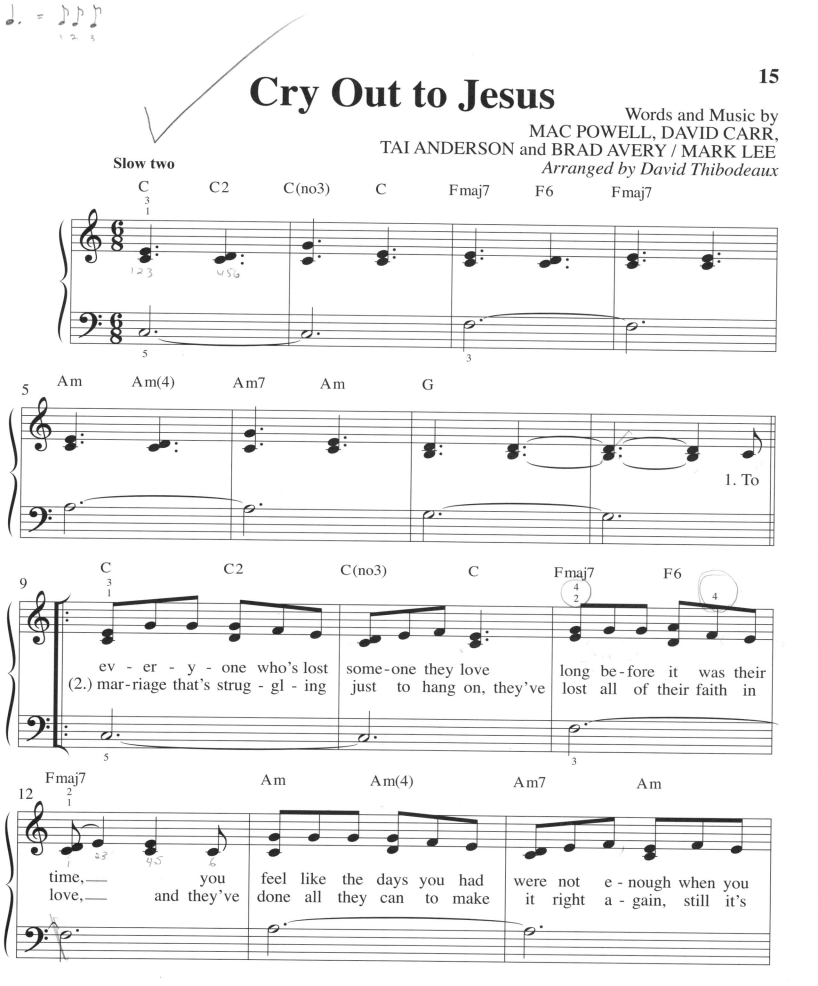

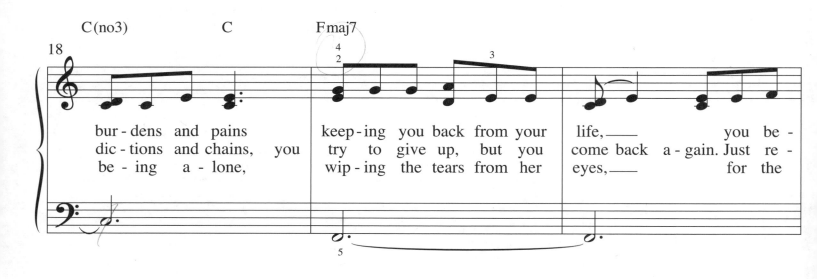

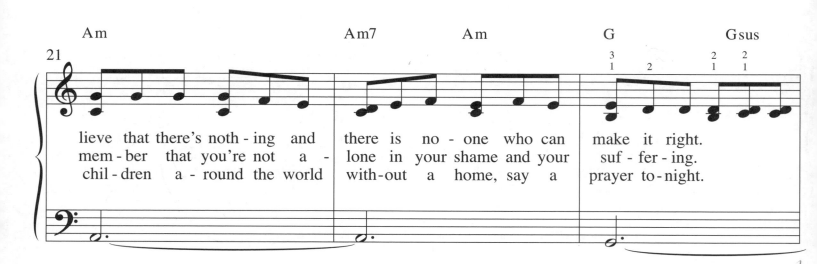

18

Friend of God

Words and Music by
ISRAEL HOUGHTON
Arranged by David Thibodeaux

22

Holy Is the Lord

Words and Music by
LOUIE GIGLIO and CHRIS TOMLIN
Arranged by David Thibodeaux

We stand and lift up our hands, for the joy of the Lord is our strength.

We bow down and wor-ship Him now. How

Holy Is Your Name

Words and Music by
MARK BYRD and STEVE HINDALONG
Arranged by David Thibodeaux

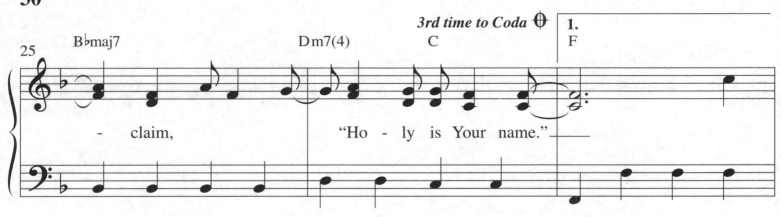

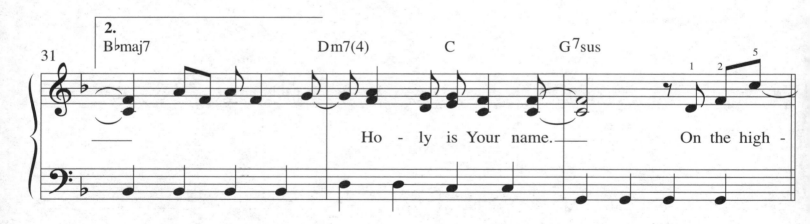

Homesick

Words and Music by
BART MILLARD
Arranged by David Thibodeaux

nev - er been more home - sick than now.

now. In Christ, there are— no good - byes. And in

Christ, there is no— end. So, I'll hold on to Je - sus with

Lifesong

Words and Music by
MARK HALL
Arranged by David Thibodeaux

My Savior, My God

Words and Music by
AARON SHUST
Arranged by David Thibodeaux

42

My God He is.— My God is al - ways gon-na be.—

— 3. Yes, liv - ing, dy - ing, let me

CODA

al-ways gon-na be.— My Sav-ior lives.— My Sav-ior loves.— My Sav-ior lives.—

— My Sav - ior loves.— My Sav - ior lives.—

How Great Is Our God

Words and Music by
ED CASH, CHRIS TOMLIN
and JESSE REEVES
Arranged by David Thibodeaux

Serious

Words and Music by
CHUCK BUTLER, SUE C. SMITH
and DAN MUCKALA
Arranged by David Thibodeaux

Do you ev-er get the feel-ing

peo-ple think you're cra-zy 'cause you trust what they can't___ see?___

Do you ev - er get the feel - in'_____

peo - ple think you're shal - low and you will change what you be - lieve? But

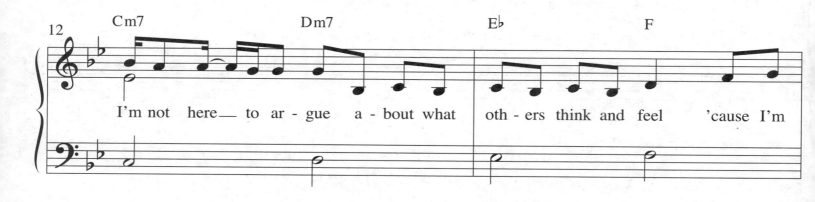

I'm not here__ to ar - gue a - bout what oth - ers think and feel 'cause I'm

not a - shamed__ to tell an - y - one_____ what I know__ to be real! I'm

2nd time to Coda ⊕

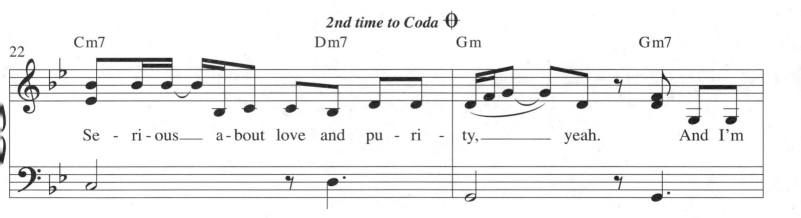

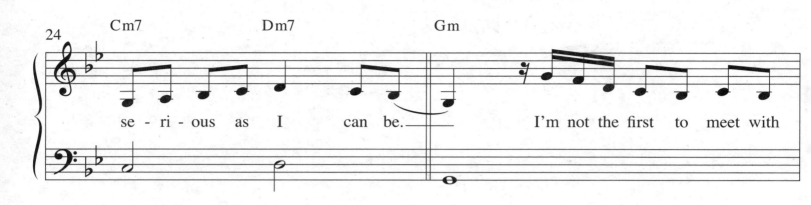

se - ri - ous as I can be. I'm not the first to meet with

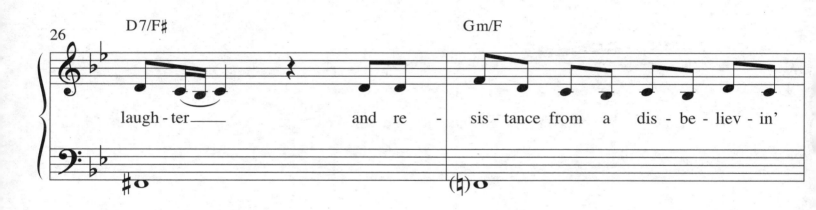

laugh - ter and re - sis - tance from a dis - be - liev - in'

crowd. But I got to meet it head on.

I'm just gon - na keep on. I won't let it get me down.

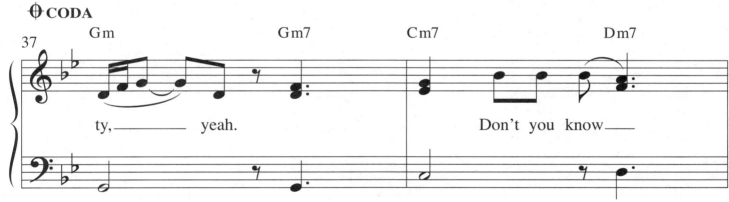

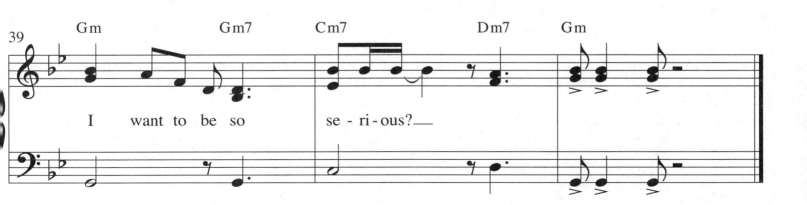

Strong Tower

Words and Music by
**MARC BYRD, MARK LEE,
JOHN SUMRALL** and **AARON SPRINKLE**
Arranged by David Thibodeaux

1. When I wan - der through the des - ert and I'm long - ing for my home, all my dreams have gone a - stray,
2. In the mid - dle of my dark - ness, in the midst of all my fear, You're my ref - uge and my hope.

when I'm strand - ed in the val -
When the storm of life is rag -

54

The Other Side of the Radio

Words and Music by
CHRIS RICE
Arranged by David Thibodeaux

58

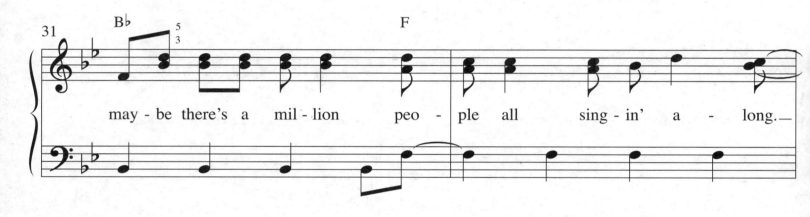

Wait for Me

Words and Music by
REBECCA ST. JAMES
Arranged by David Thibodeaux

Acoustic groove

1. Dar-lin', did you know that I, I dream a-bout you, wait-ing for the look in your eyes when we meet for the first time?___ And dar-lin', did you know that I, I pray a-bout you, pray-ing that you will hold

2. Dar-lin', did you know I dream a-bout life to-geth-er, know-ing it will be for-ev-er? I'll be yours and___ you'll be mine. And dar-lin', when I say,___ "'Til death do us part,"___ I'll mean it with all of my

62

So wait for me. Dar - lin', wait for me.

Wait for me. Wait for me. 'Cause I am

D.S. al Coda

CODA

'Cause I'm wait-ing for — you. — 'Cause I'm

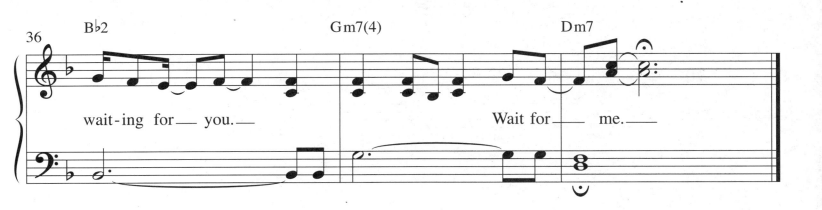

wait-ing for — you. — Wait for — me. —

Walk by Faith

Words and Music by
JEREMY CAMP
Arranged by David Thibodeaux

65

Voice of Truth

Words and Music by
STEVEN CURTIS CHAPMAN and MARK HALL
Arranged by David Thibodeaux

1. Oh, what I___ would do___ to have___ the
2. Oh, what I___ would do___ to have___ the

kind of faith___ it takes___ to climb out___ of this boat I'm in
kind of strength___ it takes___ to stand___ be-fore a gi - ant with just a

on - to the crash-ing waves, to step out of___ my com-fort zone
sling and___ a stone,___ sur - round-ed by___ the sound of a thousand

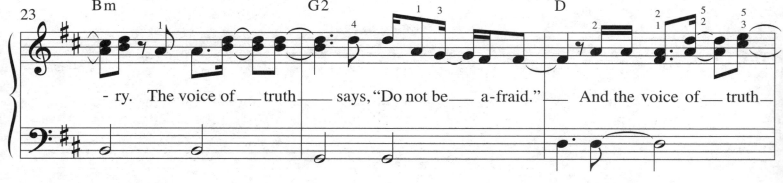